*Tumbling toward the End*

# Also by David Budbill

# DAVID BUDBILL

# Tumbling toward the End

 Copper Canyon Press
Port Townsend, Washington

Copper Canyon Press is in residence at Fort Worden State Park in Port Townsend, Washington, under the auspices of Centrum. Centrum is a gathering place for artists and creative thinkers from around the world, students of all ages and backgrounds, and audiences seeking extraordinary cultural enrichment.

LIBRARY OF CONGRESS CATALOGING-IN-PUBLICATION DATA

Names: Budbill, David, author.

Title: Tumbling toward the end / David Budbill.

Description: Port Townsend, Washington : Copper Canyon Press, [2017]

Identifiers: LCCN 2016048586 (print) | LCCN 2016056170 (ebook) | ISBN 9781556595066 (paperback) | ISBN 9781619321656 (E-book)

Subjects: | BISAC: POETRY / American / General. | LITERARY COLLECTIONS / American / General.

Classification: LCC PS3552.U346 A6 2017 (print) | LCC PS3552.U346 (ebook) | DDC 811/.54--dc23

LC record available at https://lccn.loc.gov/2016048586

COPPER CANYON PRESS

Post Office Box 271

Port Townsend, Washington 98368

www.coppercanyonpress.org

The spirit of Zen [celebrates] not the self or the seer, but the world seen.

SAM HAMILL

from the introduction to *The Poetry of Zen,* translated and edited by Sam Hamill and J.P. Seaton (Shambhala Books, 2004)

## ACKNOWLEDGMENTS

Grateful acknowledgment is made to the following magazines and anthologies for permission to reprint:

PART I

"Waiting for the Dawn": *Nine Taoist Poems* (Longhouse, 2007)

"Taoist Poet": *Nine Taoist Poems* (Longhouse, 2007)

"No Fake Mystery": *Bottle Rockets* #29 (August 2013)

"Pare Everything Down to Almost Nothing": *Bottle Rockets* #30 (February 2014)

PART II

"An Old Dog Headed for the Park": *Entelechy International: A Journal of Contemporary Ideas* #7 (2012)

"Growing Old": *Muddy River Poetry Review* #7 (Fall 2012)

"Better to Have Less": *Words Have No Meaning: Poems and Translations from the 2007 Montreal Zen Poetry Festival* (Enpuku-ji Press, 2009)

"Seventy-Two Is Not Thirty-Five": *Vermont's Local Banquet* #24 (Spring 2013)

PART III

"The Ubiquitous Daylily of July": broadside by Pressed Wafer, 2014

"Shucking Corn": *The Conium Review* (Spring 2013)

PART IV

"A Sweet Clatter" (as "Bamboo Wind Chimes"): *Bottle Rockets* #21 (2009)

"More and More Now": *Bottle Rockets* #30 (February 2014)

"Why Melancholy Beauty Is Best": *Flycatcher* #2 (January 2013)

"Foolish Monks": *Bottle Rockets* #29 (August 2013)

"Horizons Far and Near": *Nine Taoist Poems* (Longhouse, 2007)

"Shōtetsu": *Written on Water: Writings about the Allegheny River* (Mayapple Press, 2013)

"Cats": *You Must Remember This: Poems about Aging and Memory* (Poetry Society of New Hampshire, 2014)

I want to thank my wife, Lois, who reads these poems and manuscripts and who offers invaluable advice. Thanks also to my editors, Michael Wiegers and Tonaya Craft.

# CONTENTS

## Part I

## Part II

## Part III

## Part IV

*Tumbling toward the End*

## PART I

Earth's the right place for love:
I don't know where it's likely to go better.

ROBERT FROST

## Morning Meditation

Stand beside the woodstove,
hands on butt, palms turned out.
Face the window to the east.

What's left of my tea in its
capped cup stays warm on
the stove behind me.

Stare out through the window:
at sunrise, snowfall, cloudy day,
branches of the apple tree,

birds moving to and from
the dooryard feeder.
Watch the day.

Empty mind,
empty self,
into which
this poem
now comes.

# Whenever

Whenever I do the last things for the year,
like smoke the last bunch of sausages or
load the woodshed, or the first things of the
year like defrost the freezer on a subzero
night in January, as we did last night — we
put the freezer's contents out on the porch
so they'll stay colder than had they been in
the freezer at ten below — I wonder if this
will be the last time?

# This Place

> Whatever is produced by the help of another is likely to dissolve
> and perish.
>
> EKAI (1183–1260)

I came here almost fifty years ago well quit of the world, or so
I thought, and in retreat to these remote and lonely mountains
in imitation of my ancient Chinese brothers who also fled

the dark and dreck of political intrigue, the idiocies of arrogance and pretense,
    all of us
fled small minds and pompous bearing to a world of natural simplicity in
    which my
neighbors could be those who knew

the meaning of the turning seasons, of life and death, of drought
and plenty, who lived their lives and knew enough to take their dying
    seriously, who
stayed alive and faced their deaths without excuse,

who suffered and let go. I came into this place and found a life
with people who would rather see you find out, find it, for yourself than lift a
    hand to
help you, not out of arrogance or distance, but out

of modesty, respect, for your own self and for the impossibility
of ever telling anyone anything, born of their own hard-won experience,
    which has taught
them all to know that nobody

learns anything they do not need,
and seek out by themselves, to know.

# Vanity, Vanity, All Is Vanity

I'm full of aches and pains. The bottoms of my
feet hurt constantly, I've got arthritis in my
thumbs. My right arm is so weak I can't do
push-ups anymore. And I've grown hard of
hearing, but I'm too vain to get a hearing aid.

Why did this all happen to me just because
I'm growing older? Why can't I be young and
vigorous, the way I was, even though I'm old?

What makes me want what's impossible to have?
Why do I resent this thing I have become?

## Seed Order

Filling out the seed order — another
once-a-year chore like defrosting the freezer —
makes me wonder how many more times I'll
do this.

Bending or kneeling to plant has become
a problem. The pain of this simple task is almost
more than I can bear.

Yet here I am on this subzero February day
filling out the seed order again.

## On Growing Old

I'm looking for the fountain of youth too,
just like everybody else.
I never want to grow old.

We ought to give up, give in,
resign ourselves to the inevitable.
I can't. Can you?

This gnarled face,
these wrinkled hands.
What's happened to me?
I look just like my father.

## Lu Shan and Old Age

When Lu Shan was a puppy
he jumped around; he frisked.
Sometimes he jumped straight up
into the air the way lambs do.

Now he's getting older; he's nine. His
snout is white, but he still frisks with his
young friends, only the next day he can
barely move, he limps and staggers.

Just like me.

# Getting Old

Zen monk Shōtetsu
       says:
*How is it, then,*
       *that my dreams of the past*
*remain to me so clear?*

All these centuries later
       it's still true:
I can't recall
       my friend's name and I
can't remember
       what happened yesterday,

but the events
       of sixty years ago
are as vivid to me as the
       back of my wrinkled hand.

## What Is Going to Happen to Me?

I can remember clearly where I was and what I was doing
        when I was the age my daughter is now.
It was 1975 and I was thirty-five; I'd lived here on this mountainside
        for a scant four years. It's now been forty-five,
in this same house, splitting wood and bringing it in for the
        same Round Oak stove, just as I did
this morning, and as I did, I was thinking: I want to stay here,
        to the end, but I know I won't. It'll happen,
if not sooner then later. My daughter and her partner will decide
        some day that the time has come
for me to go to a nursing home. I'm writing this at the still-
        vigorous age of seventy-two. When will they
decide it's time for me to move? Will I go willingly, or will
        I put up a fight? I don't want to
give my daughter and my daughter-in-law any trouble, but
        will I be able to resist? Will I go
willingly, give up this place where I have lived and written
        for the past what will then be
almost fifty years?
        What is going to happen to me?

## Fat Chance

I can't leave this mountain.
Every time I leave,
I want to come back right away.
CH'E-HUI

I've been here almost fifty years.
I'd like to be here fifty more.
The longer I'm here the less

I want to go away. I'd like to
disappear into these mountains
and never be seen again. I don't

want to end up the way my father did,
alone and lonely in a nursing home. I
just want to do my work, make my poems,

and be left alone.
I want to stay here to the end.

## Cheery Little Ditty

Nothing you can do
will keep the juice of life
from draining away.

Shrivel, wrinkle, dry out.
Nobody is immortal.
Not even you.

People die.
It's your fate.
And once you're underground

it won't be long until
you are forgotten.

# Quoting Wang Wei without Comment

*Now Chêng and Huo were eminently fitted*
*to be included among the literati.*
*But no one cared to introduce them*
*to His Majesty.*

*Master Chêng grew old*
*with the streams and rocks;*
*Huo, the younger, dwelt quietly*
*among the hills.*

## My Friend Writes

How about a series of poems about China today?
Now that would be a challenge, as far as extracting
wisdom from idleness, soulful mellowness,
following the Tao, etc.

The reason I don't really want to go to China
is because it's all gone — what I admire, I mean.
Now they are obsessed with becoming us.

On the other hand, back then, they were such elitists,
had such a rigidly divided class system. I, given
my working-class and uneducated background,

would have been a peasant trapped in my
horrible life for all my seventy-some years.

## Pine Grosbeaks

All winter there have been
at the feeder every morning
a pair of pine grosbeaks,

both males — their red heads,
backs, and breasts contrasting with
their dark wings. They've been

mixed in with a huge flock of
redpolls — also down, these
two different kinds of brothers,

from farther north — until
this morning when
only one of them showed up.

## Winter Afternoon

The last day of February,
       a winter afternoon and
my wife has gone to town
       to shop. I bless her
for letting me stay here
       day after day, reclused
in this quiet spot.

I've been reading Kodōjin
       and napping on the couch
with the cats. I'm struck, as I often am,
       by the silence of this place.
No sounds: no cars go by on the road
       below the house, no wind,
the refrigerator doesn't run,
       only now and then
the woodstove ticks.

# How Wonderful It Is When It's Ugly Out

Late March  early April
snow            in the air
everywhere     floating
nowhere            on the
ground    gone    or
not gone    in the 20s
or the 30s    raw    cold
mean    a fire    in the
stove all day    too ugly
to go                outside
time for        soups and
stews        stay indoors
close to        the stove
at my desk    computer
making            poems

## Ars Poetica

Emerald water, emerald hills — what do they
know of ego?

...

Eyes, ears both forgotten, my body too is lost.

KODŌJIN

Poet not in poem
Poet disappeared

Gone
Self nowhere

Only eye, ear, touch, sound

reaching out
into the world

Only subject
seen and heard

## Taoist Poet

Just this
then that
then the other.

# Reply to My Peripatetic Friends

> Why would I want to go anywhere? I'm already here.
>
> LEWIS HILL, HORTICULTURIST

I go to the waterfall
and listen to the water fall.

I sit on a rock
and stare at the sky.

I watch my self disappear
into the world around me.

## Po Chü-i Believed in Idleness

Po Chü-i believed in idleness —
I might call it "staring at the wall" —

that waiting, listening for the words
of the poem to come to us,

voice of the Muse, who comes
floating to us from the other side

but only if we have that openness
to those voices only heard when we

are doing nothing, only listening
for the lady with the harp and wings

who brings us the news of the day,
that news, William Carlos Williams said,

we die from the lack of every day.

## No Fake Mystery

Say what you see.

WILLIAM CARLOS WILLIAMS

Say what you see.
Get it down right.

Accuracy is plenty.

What's here
is good enough.

# Pare Everything Down to Almost Nothing

then cut the rest,
and you've got
the poem
I'm trying to write.

# PART II

_____

I like to arrange
spring blossoms
in a rough old
funeral jar

KUAN HSIU

An Old Dog Headed for the Park
or
Glad to Have Another Day

*Montreal, March 18*


Two mornings now we've watched
    an old dog

walk past the windows of our B&B,
    out in the cold air,

out in the new snow, headed for
    the park,

yesterday with the man,
    this morning with the woman.

He's old,
    he's overweight,

he moves real slow,
    he waddles along

wagging his tail
    the whole way.

# April 15

*for Nadine*

Thirty-six years ago today
  our daughter was born.
If you focus
  on this day — here, now —
there is nothing
  to worry about.

Or so they say.

Although the garden
  is still covered with snow,
daffodils are up, red spears of tulips
  poke through,
and crocuses
  bloom in the dooryard.

## The Company of Other People

Ryōkan was an 18th- and 19th-century Japanese Zen
hermit who spent his days begging and sitting zazen.

He was also unbearably lonely almost all the time.
Often he was bored and alone and said so in his poems.

He longed for the company of other people. Like the time
he stopped at a farmer's cottage and the farmer's wife

heated sake, and the three of them sat together eating
freshly picked vegetables and talking until:

*Together, gloriously drunk, we no longer know*
*the meaning of unhappiness.*

# Ryōkan and Oppenheimer:


Ryōkan would have liked my pal Joel Oppenheimer.
Joel's been dead for more than twenty years, Ryōkan for 200.
Joel would have liked Ryōkan, too. They both liked to talk,
to sit and talk and talk, and most of the time
about nothing important. I think Ryōkan, in spite of his
Buddhist, hermit self, and because he was always lonely,
would have understood Joel's poem:

> XI
>
> *surely in buffalo*
> *there's one bar*
> *where they want us*
> *to come and sit*
> *and talk all night*
> *just a bar to talk*

## At the Imperial Tea Court

Joel and I are going to the Imperial Tea Court.
When we get there we will sip tea and look wise.

Maybe you'll see us there
drinking tea and talking.

Just two old fools
having a good time.

# Meditate on Your Own Death

It is good to meditate on your own death:
keep the image of your corpse with yourself always,
imagine your chalky bones moldering to dust,
visualize your own empty skull grinning back at you.

This way you will be able to:
intensify the joy of eating and drinking,
making love and walking, sitting in the
summer shade and visiting with friends.

## The Shadblow Tree

It's the tenth of May
      and the shadblow tree
we planted to honor
      our son's death —
he died at the age of forty —
      is in full bloom now.

It's a white cloud hovering
      at the edge of the
gardens, just as Gene
      hovers at the edge
of our lives.

## While Thinking about Death

Bitter melancholy
is better than no
melancholy at all.

## The Death of Promise Is Worse than Death

For two weeks we watched
as mother downy woodpecker

fed her young. Then today
under the apple tree I found

the rotting corpse of her young,
already insects crawling on it,

a clear liquid oozing from
its breast, its eyes a dull blue-gray

and sinking back into its head
as all of it sinks back into earth.

# Being Taught Pain

Soft as the rain
and sweet as the end of pain

ARCHIE SHEPP

About twenty years ago I began to develop a painful condition in the bottoms of my feet which has been diagnosed as "idiosyncratic peripheral neuropathy of unknown origins"; I'm not a diabetic. The condition has steadily worsened until now the bottoms of my feet are extremely painful all the time and I can't walk without severe pain. I use a cane.

A few years ago I also developed arthritis in both thumbs.

Although these problems make my life far more difficult than it used to be, I am — in an odd way — grateful for both conditions, since they let me know, in a physical way, the kind of pain so many people have to live with every day.

These conditions help me have sympathy for the suffering of the world. Don't misunderstand me, if I could get rid of these pains I would, but since I can't, I have to see these maladies as blessings, something that unites me with all who suffer.

# Growing Old

> I just don't know what this world is coming to.
> People is dying today what never died before.

MOMS MABLEY

Mary Jo Smyth is dead.
Eleanor Young is dead.
Eva Colgrove is dead.
Lu Shan is dead.

Growing old is
knowing more and
more dead people
until

you don't know
anyone at all.

## Alive and Intense

I want
to keep
as Shōtetsu did

even at an advanced age
my heart
on my sleeve

my sadness
joy
passion

as alive
and intense
as when I was young.

## Better to Have Less

The less
you have

the less
you'll lose
when it
comes time

to lose
it all.

## Anguish and Beauty

At 71, suddenly, I realize time
    is running out.

Aging and loss intensify
    the anguish and the beauty

of this life.
    Every moment becomes

more real, more important,
    more valuable.

June 4


A Blackburnian warbler hit a window
        at the back of the house
this morning. It glanced off the window
        and had just enough
consciousness left to flutter to the apple tree
        in the backyard.
It waited, rested, there until it recovered
        enough to fly away.

It's odd how these accidents, little tragedies
        in the animal kingdom,
bring us a chance to view, in this case,
        this beautiful bird:
white, yellow, black, and a brilliant,
        brilliant orange.
There's no orange in nature any brighter,
        not even oriole orange.
How lucky we are
        to see this little bird.

## In Bashō's *Travelogue*

In Bashō's *Travelogue of Weather-Beaten Bones*,
he says, *Of all the men who have entered these*
*mountains to live the reclusive life, most found*

*solace in ancient poetry.*
I wonder why he said *solace*. He must have known
how lonely and monotonous this life can be.

Don't get me wrong. Just because I said
lonely and monotonous
doesn't mean I'd trade it for anything.

I love living my life this way.

# Nobody Home

I saw an old friend at the Hardwick Area Health Center yesterday.
He shuffled in leaning on a cane, disheveled, unkempt, hair down
to his shoulders, an ancient, on his last legs. I said, "Hello," and
stupidly, "how are you?" Then I fled.

Thousands of years ago the great tombs at Maoling and Mount Li
were already lost in a wilderness of weeds. And Ozymandias, too.

Emperor Wu of the Han and the First Emperor of the Ch'in
both drank magic potions to lengthen their lives;
both died because of them. No elixir can prolong your life.

## In a Nutshell

It's me
and then
it's not me.

I am
and then
I won't be.

## Seventy-Two Is Not Thirty-Five

I spent seven hours yesterday at my daughter's house helping her expand their garden by at least ten times. We dug up sod by the shovelful, shook off the dirt as best we could; sod into the wheelbarrow and off to the pile at the edge of the yard. Then all that over and over again. Five hours' total work-time, with time out for lunch and supper. By the time I got home I knew all too well that seventy-two is not thirty-five.

I got to quit earlier than Nadine. She told me I'd done enough and that I should go get a beer and lie down on the chaise lounge and cheer her on, which is what I did.

All this made me remember my father forty years ago helping me with my garden. My father's dead now, and has been dead for many years, which is how I'll be one of these days, too. And then Nadine will help her child, who is not here yet, with her garden. Old Nadine, aching and sore, will be in my empty shoes, cheering on her own.

# Birthday

A steady gentle rain all night
      and this morning too,

temperature in the 60s,
      overcast and gray. I'm

seventy-two today. Just
      yesterday I was talking

with a friend about how much
      we love these gray and rainy

days, inside the big woods,
      just the close-in view,

only the details
      of the world nearby.

# Peony

Peony, my love,
Chinese flower,
June flower,
garish ball of
sweet perfume,
red, pink, white.

In the house a vase-full
makes the whole place
redolent of peony.

The essence of
the start of summer.

## What Is June Anyway?

After three weeks of hot weather and drought,
      we've had a week of cold and rain,
just the way it ought to be here in the north,
      in June, a fire going in the woodstove
all day long, so you can go outside in the cold
      and rain anytime and smell
the wood smoke in the air.

This is the way I love it. This is why
      I came here almost
fifty years ago. What is June anyway
      without cold and rain
and a fire going in the stove all day?

## PART III

Like following trails left by birds
who vanished with yesterday's sky.

KŌHŌ KENNICHI

## I've Given Up My Dreams of Fame and Fortune

My home is in the mountains far away.
No market forces here, nor anyone or -thing
of any importance at all.

Just clouds and trees, my woodlot,
gardens and a couple pots of tea
every afternoon.

I've given up my dreams of fame and fortune.
You can't have your cake
and eat it too.

Cut wood. Weed the beans. Make love.
Hill the potatoes.
Play a bamboo flute.

Listen for a poem.

## Rainy Day

The heat wave and drought
    are over.
The garden vegetables
    and ourselves
welcome this steady, quiet,
    all-day rain.

Cooler today, in the 50s,
    and this
gentle, sometimes not so
    gentle, rain
falling all day long.

The morning's work is over.
    Lunch is over.
Now it's time to nap,
    a rainy-day nap.

# Done


I finished cutting, splitting, stacking,
      and covering
the dead white pine that we'll use
      for kindling this
winter and next. I'm glad I'm finished.
      It's getting
hotter every day.

The woods really are
      what Frost said once,
*lovely, dark and deep.*
      And in the morning,
in the summer,
      as it is right now,
with the trees in full leaf, and the
      sun shining, there is
also, as I said once,
      *a dappled quietude of*
*irresistible tranquillity.*

# Beyond the World of Red Dust

Who never tires of my company?
Only Chingting Mountain.

LI PO

Ryōkan said,
*I see the bamboo grove*
*in front of my hut*
*a thousand times a day,*
*yet I never tire of it.*

And I never tire of
these woods and hills
on the western slopes
of Judevine Mountain,

where I have wandered
for almost fifty years
just beyond
the World of Red Dust.

And they never tire
of my company—
or at least they don't say so.

Even if they are larger than man,
mountains are his friend.

HENRY INN


I live in the mountains.
I love living here.

People ask me how I can
live so far away from

everybody, how I can live
in such a remote place.

The mountains are my friends.
Even though I can't hike

in them anymore,
I still look at them.

They are my constant
companions.

## Begin Again

Ryōkan said, *A summer night advances*
      *into chaste hours of morning.*
Would that I had said that and in that way.

I lie here sleepy-eyed looking out
      the open window as the dawn
gently overtakes the dark.

The night rain is over. Birds begin to sing.
      Through the fog and mist,
washed clean, a new day begins.

## Lu Shan's Ashes

I

Lu Shan — meaning Green Mountain —
    my all-time favorite dog,
died this spring. Yesterday, July 5, Lois and I
    took his ashes to our woods and
scattered some here and there,
    threw some in the brook
at our upper crossing, in a pool where he
    liked to wade in the summer, lie down,
cool off, and some at a four corners of our trails
    up at the top of a hill, the height of land,
where Louie always stopped, hoping for a treat,
    and then some more in the brook at the
lower crossing, near where we scattered our son's
    ashes and where our son's cairn and
black granite monument are. We'll scatter the rest
    in a few days from the float in
Wolcott Pond where Louie swam, climbed the vertical
    ladder alone, then jumped off
with complete abandon into the pond with such force
    he'd disappear completely under the water,
then pop up and race anyone audacious enough to
    challenge him or chase a ball I'd thrown
for him. All this, of course, made me wonder about
    the time when I am just a bag of ashes,
wonder who will carry me and scatter me here and there
    in the woods Lu Shan and I loved.

II

Today, July 8, we went to Wolcott Pond and scattered
       Louie's ashes from the raft.
A lot of people came for the ceremony, Louie's friends
       from as far away as Burlington
and Montreal, a flotilla of watercraft: canoes, sailboats,
       a stand-up paddleboard, all there to say
goodbye. We threw flowers into the water and handfuls
       of Lu Shan. First the ashes left a cloud
in the water, then the larger pieces glittered as they sank
       through the brackishness toward
the bottom of the pond.

## The Ubiquitous Daylily of July

There is an orange daylily that blooms in July.
It grows in everybody's dooryard — abandoned
or lived in — along the side of the road, in front of stone walls

and fences, at gas stations and garages, at the entrance to
driveways, anywhere it takes a mind to sprout. You always
see them in clusters, bunches, never by themselves. They
propagate by rhizomes, which is why they are so resilient,

and why you see them in bunches. There is an orange
daylily that blooms in July and is ubiquitous right now.
The roadside mowers mow a lot of them, but they
don't get them all. There's always some of them left.

These are not the rare and delicate lemon-yellow daylilies
or the other kinds people have around their places. This one
is coarse and ordinary, almost harsh in its weathered beauty,
like an older woman with a tough, worldly-wise and weather-

wrinkled face. It's coarse and ordinary, and beautiful because
it's coarse and ordinary, a plant gone wild and therefore
rugged, indestructible, indomitable,
resilient, like anyone or -thing has to be in order to survive.

## Hauling Stones out of the Brook

Early this morning, not long after the sun came up, I went out
to the woods to our brook to get some big, flat stones to line
the edges of the new fire pit I'm building out in front of the grape arbor,
just above the garden, where we have cookouts and campfires.

The brook is seriously low now, yet there's water to slosh around in,
and rocks to slip on. I found some nice ones: big, flat slabs of ledge,
now half buried in the brook, pieces of the ridge that looms fifty feet
above the brook just to the east, slabs broken off that ridge thousands
of years ago and tumbled slowly down into the brook over the ages.

I staggered with them up the hill over blowdowns and rocks
to the logging road where my trusty wheelbarrow waited.
The miracle of the wheelbarrow: able to haul hundreds of pounds
of stone because of the principle of the fulcrum, lever, and wheel.

When I'm pushing a wheelbarrow uphill, I'll cup my hands around
the ends of the handles, and when the going gets tough, lean forward a little
and get my gut right into the back edge of the wheelbarrow itself and push.
This, by the way, is the only advantage to a serious pot I've ever found.

But going uphill isn't nearly as tough as down.
The weight of the stones creates so much momentum I have to hold back
with all my might to keep the load from getting away.

I was covered with sweat, done and back in the house for breakfast by 7:30.
Now with a hammer and coal chisel I can modify the stones so that they'll fit
nicely around the oval edge of my new fire pit, which will be ready
for our company and campfires come July.

## After Li Po

You ask me why I live
on this green mountain.
I smile. No answer.

Come. Live here
fifty years.
You'll see.

# Summer

It's summer and I am sitting in the sun
    avoiding all
that needs to be done in the garden,
    in the woods.
Instead, I am reading Ming-dynasty poet
    Yüan Hung-tao.
In this poem he refers to
    *the old man of the*
*eastern hedge* — meaning T'ao Ch'ien —
    who wrote
more than a thousand years before
    Yüan.

Fifth century, 16th century, and me here
    in the 21st:
all three poets, all three poems,
    thinking about
chrysanthemums, the perfect flower for
    three old men.
More than 1,500 years between us, yet
    we are one,
companions — joined by our aging,
    our thoughts
of this sweet world, and our
    melancholy over leaving it.

## July 31

After a cold start, a day of sun and warmth.
It's perfectly still — no wind at all. The only sounds:
the hummingbirds moving from feeder to feeder
and the ticking of the metal roof on the house
when the sun comes out from behind a cloud.

I am here alone today, in this silence, reading
about painting, poetry, and politics in 17th-
century China — that is, when I can pay attention
to something other than this silence.

# The Sound of Summer

The screened door slamming tells me it is summer.

There are other sounds only in the summer, too.
The hummingbirds moving from
feeder to feeder on the porch, chickadee's two-note
song we hear early on summer mornings, ravens
croaking back to their aeries on the ledges
every summer evening.

There are other birds too, visitors we hear only
in the summertime, but it's the screened door slamming
that is the definition of summer for me.

## Golden Glow

August now, and sunburst, starburst, golden glow is blooming,
the traditional dooryard flower in these parts. It's just
to the right of the steps as you approach the house.

I dug up a piece of it years ago from near the old cellar hole,
which is down the lane from our house about halfway to
the road. That house, the last house on this place — until
we built ours in 1971 — burned in the 1920s.

Like the daylily and Siberian iris, golden glow propagates
by rhizomes. You've got to be careful where you put it.
You can't kill it. I've got this batch boxed in.

Every spring there is nothing in the box, and then slowly
the golden glow begins to sprout, and by the end of August
it's seven feet tall and blooming, a connection to the past.

## Shucking Corn

I was shucking corn this evening,
    about 6:30,
a gentle evening light, the air still,
    temperature
dropping. Tonight, they say, it's
    going to be
in the 40s, yet it's still early August.
    The beauty
of this evening is almost too much to bear,
    almost.
And, maybe because of that, I wonder
    how many
more summers I'll sit here shucking corn
    about 6:30
in the evening, in the still air, in this gentle
    evening light.

## Their Fall Migration Begins

This morning a little before six o'clock
      while drinking tea in bed
I saw frenetic activity
      in the white pines behind the house.

It occurred to me to wonder
      if the fall wood warbler migration
had begun. I got the binoculars,
      but by then the birds were, as usual, gone.

It's only August 12
      but it's time to go, or so say those
little birds. We may not be ready,
      but they are: which means south,

to Central America, Mexico, the West Indies,
      for the winter,
including, I hope, the Blackburnian warbler
      who hit the window last spring.

Flying mostly at night, they'll all be gone
      by the end of next month.

## It's August

It's August and all I can think about
is what it will be like after Labor Day.
Think of it: soon: nothing to do, nowhere
to go, nobody to see. Oh! just think of it!

All that emptiness into which I can pour
whatever it is I might want to see and say.
Emptiness. Blessed emptiness.

Then a little voice says,
*But when I get it, I don't know*
*what to do with it, and then*
*I wish I didn't have it.*

## Toward the End of August

Toward the end of August I begin to dream about fall, how
this place will empty of people, the air will get cold and
leaves begin to turn. Everything will quiet down, everything
will become a skeleton of its summer self. Toward

the end of August I get nostalgic for what's to come, for
that quiet time, time alone, peace and stillness, calm, all
those things the summer doesn't have. The woodshed is
already full, the kindling's in, the last of the garden soon

will be harvested, and then there will be nothing left to do
but watch fall play itself out, the earth freeze, winter come.

# The End of August

Hot. Really hot. We spent
      the afternoon swimming
in the pond to soothe our sweaty
      bodies. Now, it's
evening and we are all around
      the campfire out near
the grape arbor. We can feel
      the cold air spilling down
the sidehill all around us. We move
      closer to the fire.
It's cold now. The end of August.
      Autumn is in the air.

The Man Who Tries Not to Be Busy Speaks
or
Trying to Explain the Life of a Poet

*after a poem by Robert Bly*


I don't want to run around.
I don't want to travel.
I don't want to have things to do.
I don't want to be busy.

I want to stay in one place.
I want to do the same thing every day.
I want to daydream.
I want to stare at the wall.
I want to do nothing.

## August 24

I was right.
The fall migration has begun.
I know because, unfortunately,
this morning a wood warbler
hit a window in my wife's studio
and knocked himself out.
I went outside, picked him up and
as soon as I did he began
to squirm and struggle,
which is a good sign.
I put him in the backyard apple tree
on the same branch where
this spring on June 4
another warbler recovered.

After about an hour, he was gone.

## In Those Tiny Brains


Toward the end of August
    I begin to wonder what's going on
with the hummingbirds,
    what's going on in those tiny brains.

When do they start to feel strange,
    that pull to leave, go south?

They've got a long trip ahead of them,
    all the way to Central America.

By the beginning of September they'll be gone,
    but when does the urge begin?

Does it build slowly
    or is it all of a sudden, one day?

# Late August

Asters bloom.
Leaves begin to turn.
Kestrels on the power lines.
Time to get in wood.

# Invisible Visitors

All through August and September
        thousands, maybe
tens of thousands, of feathered
        creatures pass through
this place and I almost never see
        a single one. The fall
wood warbler migration goes by here
        every year, all of them,
myriad species, all looking sort of like
        each other, yellow, brown, gray,
all muted versions of their summer selves,
        almost indistinguishable
from each other, at least to me, although
        definitely not to each other,
all flying by, mostly at night, calling to each
        other as they go to keep
the flock together, saying: chip, zeet,
        buzz, smack, zip, squeak—
those sounds reassuring that we are
        all here together and
heading south, all of us just passing
        through, just passing
through, just passing through, just
        passing through.

# PART IV

Direct statement of acutely perceived experience is in general
more moving.

HAYDEN CARRUTH

# After Labor Day

*for Bill Porter*


Fall is coming. Kodōjin says,
*Hermits love autumn best.*
Soon the cold will be here.
We'll have a fire in the woodstove
every day. We'll sit beside the stove
with a *wee dram of Scotch* and enjoy
the silence and the emptiness together.

## Hermit Thrush

Just at dawn and then again at dusk
for only a couple of days this time of year

in the dooryard apple tree:
a number of hermit thrushes.

These birds migrate at night. They are either
ending a nighttime flight from the north

or about to begin one to the south, or both.
But right now they are resting and feeding.

For some reason they love the blossoms on the
fuchsia that hangs from that dooryard apple tree.

We hear them all summer in the deep woods,
but they are secretive birds so we never see them.

They are silent now. It's nice to see these visitors
in our apple tree now that they are on their way

to Central America. *Bon voyage, little round birds.*
*I hope we hear and later see you again next year.*

# Dragonfly, Darning Needle, Mosquito Hawk

By the middle of August almost all
the biting insects are gone;
then comes one last infestation:
mosquitoes
just before the first killing frost.

It's September now
and every evening the air is full of
dragonflies, darning needles, mosquito hawks,
as they go about the business of eating all those
recently hatched mosquitoes:
this dance of death.

## The Last Peach

During the last part of the summer
    we're able to get
Pennsylvania Amish peaches, a rare
    treat here in the
north country. Every morning we have
    them on our cereal.
We eat them every way we can, but
    mostly we eat them
raw. What's better than a firm, juicy
    peach;
your mouth filled with sweet juice,
    juice running down your chin?
But today, four days into September, alas!
    we ate the last one for this year.
We do not buy peaches in the grocery store,
    canned or otherwise, nor do we
buy them any time of the year, except
    when we can get fresh Amish peaches.

We ate the last one for breakfast
    this morning:
a harbinger of fall, a sign,
    just like kestrels
on the power lines,
    asters blooming,
and hummingbirds leaving.

## The White Pine Tree

The white pine tree that stands
    between the house and garden
was a little tree forty-five years ago,
    six inches in diameter, at the most.

Now, a lifetime later, and still growing,
    the white pine tree
reaches up and out. It's almost three feet
    in diameter on the stump,
about fifty feet tall and its branches span
    at least thirty feet.

I see it now, outlined in morning light,
    as if it wore a halo, and I marvel
at what this living thing — which has been
    a part of my life every day
for almost forty-five years —
    has become.

## All-Night September Rain

An early September night and still warm.
I get in bed with the window open, then
turn off the lights and listen to the rain.

Five o'clock in the morning and still dark,
still warm, window still open, sound
of rain still comes down through the dark.

Summer's over, garden's tired, harvest is
almost over, something special, strange,
mysterious about this all-night September rain.

## Hummingbirds All Summer

The real beginning of fall is the day the hummingbirds leave. This year it was September 5, two days after Labor Day. Or maybe it was the 4th or the 6th, but by the 7th we knew they were gone. There's still a hummingbird or two now and then at the feeders, but they're transients, just passing through, who stop here for a snack on their way to Central America.

With the hummingbirds gone it gets quieter. And with the bugs gone too, the world is definitely more silent. The last of the warblers are passing through now but mostly at night, so we almost never hear or see them. And when the songbirds go, and all the leaves come down, this really will be an empty place.

Toward the middle of May, one of us will be at the sink, when suddenly outside the kitchen window there is a tiny bird squeaking at us and saying, *We're back from Costa Rica. Get out the feeders.* This proves to us that we get the same birds year after year. How else would they know to come to our window to tell us they are back? We obey and make some syrup — four-parts water, one-part sugar, bring it to a boil to make sure the sugar is in solution, cool it, put it in the feeders, hang the feeders up and summer begins.

All summer hummingbirds zoom back and forth between the dooryard apple tree and the two feeders — one hanging from a used chainsaw file nailed to the corner of the house, the other from a nail on the corner of the woodshed.

There's always a period early in the summer when the birds disappear, more or less, for a couple of weeks, after which, when they return, their population has doubled or tripled. We can tell the young ones from the parents by their size and their behavior.

So it goes, all summer, these tiny, exuberant, belligerent birds who entertain us all day long until that day they leave us without even saying goodbye.

## A Sweet Clatter

The bamboo wind chimes
in the dooryard apple tree

make a sweet clatter
in the autumn wind.

## September Light

Mid-September and the setting sun illuminates the 50-foot
white pine tree that stands between the house and garden.
I can see parts of the tree I never see any other time of

the day or year. The inner branches blaze orange and gold
in the setting sun. Through an absolutely clear, blue sky
a jet, bright and brilliant silver in the setting sun, goes over

the top of the tree at 30,000 feet. Today's half-moon is
to the right, and by the time I write this the jet has gone
under the moon and disappeared. When I turn again to look,

the light — once all orange and gold — is gone, and the tree is
again its ordinary, usual, impenetrable, green self.

# A Mid-September Pot of Flowers

Overflowing, hanging off the edge, out and down,
a mid-September pot of flowers on the porch railing
doesn't know — or doesn't care — its life is almost over.

Hundreds of little petunia blossoms, five fused fuchsia
petals with deep-set, bright-yellow centers, the kind
right now a honeybee — from our neighbor's hives —
climbs right into and almost disappears.

Then suddenly a hummingbird; not one of ours — they
have gone — but a migrant, transient, just stopping by
for a quick snack on its way to South America.

In the pot also a few bright-yellow pansies. Nearby its
cousin, purple, yellow, almost white — Johnny-jump-ups,
the perfect name for this volunteer, come-from-out-of-
nowhere flower.

Oh! look, see what's here!
So beautiful, so temporary,
like you and me.

## More and More Now

I want to say
less and less

chickadee
buttercup squash

firewood
maple leaves

chrysanthemum

# Dahlias

Dahlias at the corner of
      the porch railing.
This one:
      deep green foliage,
round red blossoms,
      Chinese red.
Red-orange circles,
      multipetaled
yellow centers,
      blooming profusely
in the autumn sun.

## Summer Pasta

The real end of summer isn't when the hummingbirds leave; it's the last time we have Summer Pasta, meaning: a fresh tomato sauce. Tomatoes peeled, chopped, and drained. (Save the juice to drink later: add celery seed, salt and pepper, stir vigorously and chill.) Grate some Parmesan into a bowl — it should be freshly grated. Put that on the table, along with a bowl of freshly chopped cilantro.

When the chopped tomatoes have drained in the colander awhile, and you have stirred them with your hands a few times, simmer three or four dry chili peppers in olive oil. After a while, add a lot of slivered garlic — the more, the better. Let the garlic cook until it's golden brown and chewy, so that it sticks to your teeth. Put the drained tomatoes in a serving bowl and mix in some chopped fresh parsley and basil. Pour hot oil and garlic over the tomatoes, parsley, and basil. Toss. Add a little salt and pepper. People at the table can add more.

Cook some pasta. My favorite is capellini (extra-thin spaghetti) but it doesn't work so well with chunks of tomato, so instead use fusilli (curlicues), chiocciole (small shells), or penne rigate (small tubes). Use a mix of whole wheat and semolina pasta.

When the pasta is a little more done than al dente drain and toss with the fresh tomatoes, hot oil, garlic, parsley, and basil. Serve with Parmesan, chopped cilantro, salt and pepper, and copious amounts of red wine.

## Why Melancholy Beauty Is Best

In ancient China all you had to do
     was say *chrysanthemum.*
Everybody got sad, sighed, and
     suddenly became melancholy.

Now here they are,
     three pots of them
on the porch: yellow, white,
     and copper-beech brown.

October.
     Sky clear.
Sun warm.
     A riot of color in the hills.

This afternoon we'll drink
     chrysanthemum tea and sigh
for all this momentary,
     melancholy beauty.

# The Party

Our neighbors, Frank and Eva Colgrove, true hill farmers, whom we first met forty-five years ago, have both died. They were the real thing: heated with wood, milked about fifteen Jersey cows, had a huge garden, raised a pig, ate the cows as they came off the line, sugared, and Eva put everything by, two big freezers' worth, plus she canned everything you can think of, including wild cranberry jelly—cranberries she picked herself down in the swamp—and headcheese made from the meat of a pig's skull, and dandelion wine too.

When Frank and Eva's went up for sale, we imagined the worst: since the place is so beautiful, somebody would make a killing on the farm, and wouldn't it be perfect for a bunch of condos. Luckily the economy tanked and Jim came along and bought the place. Three years ago, Jim and his partner, Katie, started an organic farm: cows, pigs, chickens, two greenhouses, and every kind of vegetable you can think of.

It feels strange now to be the old couple up the road.

They had a big party this past weekend out back of the house for their patrons, neighbors, and friends. Lots of people came, from babes in arms to eighty-five-year-olds. Potluck. Tons of great food, headlined by crock-pots full of pulled pork and baked beans; and after dark strings of little white lights gracefully looped everywhere outdoors, and tents out in the field for those spending the night, and an enormous bonfire and a band that played well into the next day.

## Envoy to the Party

It was eight thirty or quarter to nine when we left. The band
had played only a few tunes. I used to be a terrific dancer.
In the past I would have never left early. I know my wife
was disappointed that we were leaving — she's a
serious dancer also — but my feet, as usual, were killing me.

When we got home — we are Jim and Katie's nearest neighbors,
half a mile away — we could still hear the band. While I was
downstairs sleeping, Lois was upstairs with the window open listening to
          the music,
which, because of me, she had to leave.

## Cleaning the Cellar

A few days ago I was cleaning the cellar and back in a far corner
I found my old minnow trap that I hadn't seen in maybe thirty years.

Inside the trap was the skeleton, with a little hide attached, of
a mouse who had gotten into the trap and couldn't get out.

The mouse was right near the entrance and clearly trying to get out when he
        finally died
of starvation. How long was he in the trap trying

to get out? How many days of slowly starving to death? All of his teeth were
        still in his
skeleton head. His mouth was open in a scream.

What haunts me more than anything is the look on his face.
It was a human look.

## Smoking the Last Batch of Sausages for the Year

Every year in October, I smoke a smoker-full of hot and sweet Italian
sausages so that we can freeze them and put them all winter in
our red sauce with onions and green peppers.

This year on that evening the sky was clear, the sunset beautiful.
I sat in my plastic chair — in the chill autumn light, in the afterglow —
and drank my beer. It was cold, but nowhere near a frost.

I watched my greasy charges engulfed in smoke. As dark came
on, I thought about how every year getting ready for winter is
one last thing after another, and here was yet another annual
ritual engaged in, completed.

It was completely dark — except for the few remaining coals glowing
red in the smoker and the moon just beginning through the trees —
when the sausages and I were done.

## Antipoems and Cordwood

All these crazy
        antipoems
stack up like
        the firewood
I'm forever
        cutting.

## Not That Much Has Changed

Shōtetsu saw a bundle of firewood
    coming down the mountain
        on a woodsman's back.

My neighbor, his son, and I haul my firewood
    out of the woods and home
        with his tractor and wagon.

In some ways, not that much has changed
    in the last
        seven hundred years.

## Loading the Woodshed — 2012

I finished loading the woodshed today. Every year
I tell myself, *This is it, the last time. It's just too*
*much work, too painful, and I'm too old.*
And then, the next year, when fall rolls
around, the air gets cold, and the geese go south, I
load the woodshed again.

How long will this go on? I'm seventy-two.
Every year it takes me longer to recover,
yet every year I keep doing it.

It's just, now that I'm done, I can go out into
the woodshed, sit in a chair, and look at all those
neatly stacked rows, six and a half feet high, six feet
long and sixteen inches deep, two sets of rows like that,
left and right, four full cord — not much by some standards —
but enough to keep us warm all winter.

When I go out and look at what I've done, I get such a deep
sense of satisfaction from this backaching labor that I can't
imagine a year without going through all that pain again.

## Ready for Winter

Woodshed's full of dry wood.
Kindling's put up.
Parsley and rosemary
potted and inside.
A pile of well-rotted manure
on top of every rhubarb crown.
The garden tilled and resting.
Next year's wood cut,
stacked, and covered
out in the woods.
Drive staked and flagged.
Cellar closed.

# Old Fool

*for Steve Sanfield*


Sprained my back
stacking firewood.

Always a fool.


Now an old fool.

# Foolish Monks

*for Steve Sanfield*

Ryōkan said:
>    *Last year, a foolish monk;*
>    *This year, no change!*

You can add me to that list,
and also my friend Steve.

## Loading the Woodshed — 2013

This is the first year in the last forty-five that I have not loaded the wood-shed myself. I am seventy-three this year. The peripheral neuropathy in the bottoms of my feet and the arthritis in my hands have gotten so bad I can't do it anymore. I hire it done: the wood cut, stacked, and covered last year, then this fall, split and trucked to the woodshed and stacked again. I have a friend in New Jersey, a few years younger than I am, who called the other day to ask if I was still cutting my own wood and load-ing the woodshed myself.

He was relieved to find out I hire it done now. He stacks a cord of wood on the front porch of his suburban house in his suburban town and finds that increasingly painful.

We all grow old and have to give up things we did when we were young. There is grief and sadness when something you've done for so long comes to an end.

# Variation on a Late-Fall Theme

As November approaches
all I can think about is winter,

living in and through the cold,
close to my woodstove.

No more chores or deadlines,
projects or requirements, rather

emptiness, quiet, time to sleep,
space to listen for the voices from

within.

## Horizons Far and Near

Why am I so happy here on Judevine Mountain?
My friends say I should travel, see the world.

They say I would improve myself, broaden my
perspectives, expand my horizons. Why can't

they understand I don't want to travel anywhere
except out into my woods, down the hill across

the brook and up into the stand of big white pine
about half a mile from here.

## Six Horses

Six horses in a corner of a field, in their winter coats,
shaggy jowls, all standing together in the late-October sun.

Fifty-seven degrees, tails still, no flies to swish, all of them basking
in this rare day, this warmth and sun, all of them quiet

enjoying the heat on their hides. All of us saying,
*Oh! it is good to be alive on this late-October day.*

## Cold Weather's Here

At ten o'clock every morning,
    four hours after getting up,
two hours after breakfast,
    I make a pot of kukicha.

A small cup for my wife,
    the rest for me,
and back to work at my desk
    upstairs in my room.

# What I Saw This Morning

His hands jammed deep into the pockets of his jeans,
        shoulders up around his ears —
it's cold this morning — a young man waits to
        cross the road, go to the store,
for coffee, a doughnut, or maybe a pakora,
        which the Indian family who run the store
make: *But only in the morning-time.*

Thirty years ago, or sixty, other men stood
        in this same place, hands jammed
into their pockets, shoulders up around their ears.
        Now those guys are dead,
and this young man is here to take his turn.

# Trying to Laugh at Myself


Pickup says
*Partial to pine cliffs and lonely trails*
*an old man laughs at himself when he falters.*

Fifty years ago
I would not have understood those lines.
Now I try to laugh as I try to get up.

# Among but Not With

Trying to follow the Tao
      I went north
into the mountains
      at the age of 29,
just as and when
      Han Shan did,
to live among simple
      people like myself.

I wanted to go, as Frost said,
      *into my own,*
live among but not with
      other people,
live in the mountains,
      build a house,
cut wood, garden
      alone with only
my wife, a cat, a dog,
      and
the limitless woods
      for company.

# Incident

Almost fifty years ago, when I came to Judevine Mountain,
I put away my date book. Days and months flowed by like the river.
I followed a calendar no smaller than the seasons.

Then one gray and wet November day, on a high plateau,
where open fields stretched away on both sides of the road,
while I drove a tractor and a wagon down off Judevine Mountain,
something compelled me to stop and wait.

After a while, a man climbed out of my chest, and down off
the tractor. He straightened his tie, picked up his briefcase,
looked at me quizzically, smiled, nodded, stepped across the road
into a brown field, and hurried off toward the woods.

I watched until he disappeared,
started the tractor again, and
drove off into the rest of my life.

# When the Tamaracks Turn Yellow

When the tamaracks turn yellow
and the mountaintops are white,

after all the tourists have gone away —
because they think there is nothing left

to see — then those of us who stay, we
hunker down in sweet silence,

blessed emptiness, and
get ready for the coming snow.

## Shōtetsu

Shōtetsu saw the wind ripple the surface
of a stream as it flowed through a meadow.

He also saw the wrinkles of his own face
reflected in the surface of the stream.

## A Poem about Pain

I can feel myself slipping away, fading away, withdrawing
from this life, just as my father did. When the pain you're in

is so great you can't think about or pay attention to anything
but your own pain, the rest of the world and all other life

don't matter.

I think about my friends with dementia, cancer, arthritis, and
how much more pain they are in than I am, but it does no good,

their pain is not mine, and therefore, no matter how magnanimous
I might want to be, their pain is not as important to me as my own.

## I Never Thought This Would Come to Me

Because I'm seventy-five and have a rare form of Parkinson's disease
I can't cut wood anymore, nor can I mow. And I can't garden
    anymore either.

As my father used do say, *I never thought*
    *this would come to me.*

## Another Poem about Pain

> Ill health is likely to breed ill thoughts.
>
> RYŌKAN

*And Ryōkan ought to know, he being so sickly all his adult life.*

Sometimes pain interferes with gratitude.
I wish it weren't true, but sometimes it is.
Pain makes the mind, the self, so foggy

you can't pay attention to anything but
the pain. Sometimes all you want to do
is lie down and never get up, which isn't

quite the same as dead, but almost. The
question then is: how can you maintain
your gratitude for this life, when you can't

pay attention to anything but your pain?

## He Grieves

He grieves to see his hair turn white

HAN SHAN

He grieves over thoughts of what might have been.
He grieves to see his flesh wrinkle and sag.
He grieves to see his flesh crumple and flake off.
He grieves at losing the power to attract women.
He grieves at not being able to do the things he once did.
He grieves every morning over how much his body hurts.
Such is the grief of a man growing old.

# No

Don't give me any answers
I don't want any answers
I only want to feel my grief

## Hope for the Agèd

My friend, Sigh, sent me a video of Von Freeman,
          the tenor saxophonist,
playing "Bewitched, Bothered and Bewildered."

You remember Von,
          he's Chico's daddy. Von will be ninety next year.
He plays the tune

incredibly slowly, and just a hair behind the beat,
          paying attention
to each note. And this after a lifetime of flying

          through tunes
and their changes so fast lightning had trouble
          keeping up.

Von Freeman lovingly forms every note. I thought
          of Duke Ellington
saying, "A man's sound is his total personality."

          There Von Freeman is,
standing up, his horn in his mouth, looking like
          a million bucks,

and he a year away from ninety.
          Von died on August 11, 2012,
shortly after I wrote this poem.

## Goodbye to the Road

No more touring
        or performing.
Withdraw, pull in,
        stay home.

No more contact
        with the outside world.
Only me and this world,
        these trees, this

mountainside,
        insular, withdrawn,
right here
        at home.

## An End to It

When I came to this mountainside almost fifty years ago it never oc-
curred to me that there would be an end to it.

I went along never thinking about the time when I would have to
quit. I imagined — I guess — all this would last forever, if I imagined it at
all. Now I'm in my seventies and all I can think about is the time when
my life here will be no more.

For example, I love being in the woods felling and bucking hard-
wood trees, stacking and covering the blocks, then a year or two later,
hauling them to the woodshed where I stack them again, and split them
all winter long into the right size for the weather — then bring them into
the house.

Now this chore I love so much is seriously painful, and I can see,
now, an end to it.

# I Don't Want to Leave This World

As I said once, *In spite of all*
*that could be wrong and is:*

I don't want to leave this world.
I want to keep doing what I do here every day.
I want to stay home, go to my room,
and tinker with some poems.

I like it here.
I don't want to go away.

## Cats

I wrote a poem once in which I talked about
how our cats often went to the woods to die,

then, not able to pull it off, they'd come home
to eat and sleep, wait for another opportunity.

Eventually, and inevitably, there's a one-way trip
to the woods. Half the poems I write these days

are about death. Yet here I am at it still, again,
even after this book-full of mournful poems. I'm

like our cats. I'm back to eat and sleep… and write
some more. No one-way trip for me either… yet.

## Waiting for the Dawn

I got up in the middle of the night,
put a few more chunks of wood

in the stove, stood and watched
the fire for a moment, then closed

the door, sat down in the dark and
quiet house and waited for the dawn.

# About the Author

David Budbill (1940–2016) was born in Cleveland, Ohio to a streetcar driver and a minister's daughter. He is the author of eight books of poems, seven plays, two novels, a collection of short stories, two picture books for children, and the libretto for an opera. During his prolific career David performed his work in many venues — from schools and prisons in Vermont to avant-garde performance spaces in New York City — often with William Parker and other musical collaborators. David lived a humble, engaged, and passionate life in the green mountains of Vermont with his wife of 50 years, the painter Lois Eby.

Poetry is vital to language and living. Since 1972, Copper Canyon Press
has published extraordinary poetry from around the world to engage
the imaginations and intellects of readers, writers, booksellers,
librarians, teachers, students, and donors.

**WE ARE GRATEFUL FOR THE MAJOR SUPPORT PROVIDED BY:**

THE PAUL G. ALLEN
FAMILY FOUNDATION

Anonymous
Jill Baker and Jeffrey Bishop
Donna and Matt Bellew
John Branch
Diana Broze
Sarah and Tim Cavanaugh
Janet and Les Cox
Catherine Eaton and David Skinner
Mimi Gardner Gates
Linda Gerrard and Walter Parsons
Gull Industries, Inc.
on behalf of William and Ruth True
The Trust of Warren A. Gummow
Elizabeth Hebert
Steven Myron Holl
Lakeside Industries, Inc.
on behalf of Jeanne Marie Lee

TO LEARN MORE ABOUT UNDERWRITING
COPPER CANYON PRESS TITLES,
PLEASE CALL 360-385-4925 EXT. 103

WE ARE GRATEFUL FOR THE MAJOR SUPPORT PROVIDED BY:

Maureen Lee and Mark Busto

Rhoady Lee and Alan Gartenhaus

Ellie Mathews and Carl Youngmann as The North Press

Anne O'Donnell and John Phillips

Suzie Rapp and Mark Hamilton

Joseph C. Roberts

Jill and Bill Ruckelshaus

Cynthia Lovelace Sears and Frank Buxton

Kim and Jeff Seely

Dan Waggoner

Austin Walters

Barbara and Charles Wright

The dedicated interns and faithful volunteers

of Copper Canyon Press

The Chinese character for poetry is made up of two parts: "word" and "temple." It also serves as pressmark for Copper Canyon Press.

This book is set in Minion, designed for digital composition by Robert Slimbach in 1989. Display type is set in Quadraat, designed by Fred Smeijers. Book design and composition by VJB/Scribe.